to Sue
my favorite
intellectual

love,
Jim

PROFITABLE COEXISTENCE

A NEW STRATEGY IN FOREIGN AFFAIRS

PROFITABLE COEXISTENCE

A NEW STRATEGY IN FOREIGN AFFAIRS

JAMES D. BLUM

Rutledge Books, Inc.

Danbury, CT

Copyright© 1998 by James D. Blum

Rutledge Books, Inc.
107 Mill Plain Road, Danbury, CT 06811
1-800-278-8533

Manufactured in the United States of America

Cataloging in Publication Data
Blum, James D.
    Profitable coexistence

    ISBN: 1-887750-74-6

    1. International economic relations.   2. Economic history —
1971- 3. Economic development — Environmental aspects.

363.7   97-69937

CONTENTS

INTRODUCTION

THE WORLD HAS DRIFTED PAST the Cold War era. How shall we make a better world?

This short book will touch lightly on a new approach.

At the end of the Twentieth Century, there is no "Maginot line" left in any area or field of endeavor. Knowledge can never be hemmed in again. For this fact, we should be grateful.

Now is the time to seize on ideas and strategies that can bring nations and peoples together, not for eternal love but so as to coexist in a sustainable way. Gone is the era of the grand technological solution or miracle weapon which, in the words of the immortal United States Secretary of Defense, can end all problems at a date certain or at the end of whatever year.

The basis for the world modus vivendi is already in place. It is the post-World War II "World Economic Club", an intertwining of economies through trade, financial dealings and the development of new technologies, particularly in the information and telecommunications areas.

After the fall of the Roman Empire, the Roman commercial

law continued by custom in the Mediterranean area for nearly one thousand years. Today's world economic order is a much more pervasive and powerful force.

The current system of nation-states will not give way any time soon to a new international political order. Rather, we have entered a retrograde era of ethnic conflicts which rattle the foundations of the nation-state itself. Nations-states can barely keep up with the advancement of technologies in the corporations. Organized criminal groups around the globe link arms to undermine governmental authority. Influxes of refugees upset the internal balance of nations.

How can nations collectively wield the positive forces at their command to direct international affairs on a more sustainable course? We need to examine these positive forces in a thorough way which takes nothing for granted.

The massive techno-economic linkage created by the free economic order since World War II constitutes a "critical mass". It is the power to create industries and then to replace them with newer, more competitive industries. It is the ability to create newer, more ecologically-sound industries to replace the old polluters. It is the power to achieve economic change without political disorder. Its awesome hand is more powerful than any governmental authority, and its boiler is fired by masses of information.

Membership in this "world economic club" is the most powerful incentive for peace that exists today or at any time in history. To stay out of the club is to guarantee impoverishment and stagnation in an era of rising expectations throughout the globe. Staying out — or what the economists call "autarky" — is no longer a viable option. Even the Serbian President Milosevic would have to agree with that statement.

The more rigid and "traditional" the society or ruling structure of a country, the more likely that free information flow is a problem. For these countries, change can only be accomplished incrementally. We must come up with ways to help these societies cope with the contemporary pulse of international interchange. They must come to realize that there is no road back to an earlier era.

The craft of international statesmanship in the Twenty-first Century must aim to wrap all nations as tightly as possible into the "world economic club". Maximum co-dependence and reduction of barriers of every sort are the main means to achieve this goal. At the same time, it is of vital importance to concentrate the necessary resources to determine how to most effectively assist the poorest countries as well as those groups in the advanced societies bypassed by the economic change. All we can know for sure is that the pace of change is likely to quicken.

The potential for improvement in international relations is only limited by our imaginations.

"What limits you?" proclaimed a young Chinese woman who had just experienced the horrors of the Cultural

Revolution, upon her first encounter with Western (United States) society. What limits any society? One answer is: if a society has to spend the bulk of its wealth for self-defense, self-censorship or for any other means of control, then progress will be insufficient. However, if nations can become able to survive and coexist in an atmosphere of openness, or at least make progress in that direction, then there is no limit to the possible accomplishments beyond technical and economic limitations.

Diversity is the core ingredient for healthy international relations in the Twenty-first Century. Uniformity has never been the friend of evolution or international relations. One of the famous stories from the era of the great "Dust Bowl" in the United States' Midwest during the 1930s economic depression told of one farmer who found one stalk of wheat in his field which survived the terrible blight. From that one stalk comes the bread that we eat today.

"What limits you?" is really the ultimate question. Why does a society fail? The laws of economic competition care not one bit for societal limitations. Ultimately, countries will have to overcome these malaises in order to remain competitive in the world economy. This is the inseparable link between politics and economics.

The system of "floating exchange rates" shelters countries so that they can pursue their preferred social policies, but only up to a certain point. A currency can only fall so far before the dysfunctional country falls by the wayside. In this way, the price of a currency under freely floating exchange rates is a key measure of a country's failure or success.

The economic "facts on the ground" have an impact beyond all the strategizing generals and Machiavellian schemers.

When a society with no natural resources other than the talents of its people can outshine another with the world's most advanced weaponry, then the obvious questions is: what is the true source of power?

This writer's answer is: the society that has the knowledge and intelligence to exercise restraint in its affairs and which pursues its economic well-being in concert with other nations in an atmosphere of openness.

CHAPTER ONE

TRAGEDIES CAN LEAVE IN THEIR wake the hope for renewal. The experience of Southeast Asia after the fall of South Vietnam in 1975 is instructive in this regard.

The reunification of Vietnam under the forces of the North caused a new state of affairs to take hold in Southeast Asia. It was not the collapse of dominoes. Rather, it was a loud economic hum. Let us take a brief look at what happened.

The end of Vietnam's struggle brought forth daunting economic realities. As revolutionary ardor gave way to economic realization, Vietnams' leaders had to accept the necessity to achieve greater interchange with the rest of the world.

Under any political authority, Vietnam is a diverse and unmanageable country. The imposition of ideologies-Communist, Confucian or Capitalist — can only be at the minimum imperfect. The terrain, climate and regional variations are daunting. Imperial rescripts and Communist manifestoes are no match for the realities.

What were the forces which led to Vietnam's integration

into the new, dynamic Southeast Asia? Why did Southeast Asia pull together so well after the end of the United States involvement in Vietnam? What are the lessons for the rest of the world?

All the recriminations in the United States after the fall of Saigon in 1975 cannot change one basic fact: it is futile to intervene in another country's civil war.

When the United States pulled into its shell after the fall of Saigon, the nations of Southeast Asia banded together as never before to bridge their differences under the banner of ASEAN, the Association of Southeast Asian Nations. Hemmed in from the north by China and still part of the Cold War battleground as a result of Vietnam's alliance with the Soviet Union, the risks were immense.

The collapse of the American-supported government of General Lon Nol in Cambodia to the Khmer Rouge forces added a further destabilizing element to the situation. The Khmer Rouge murdered two million of the most educated Cambodian citizens, destroyed the economy and the basic infrastructure, and launched border raids against Vietnam, based on ancient territorial claims.

When Vietnam used the Khmer Rouge raids as a pretext for intervention in Cambodia, the specter of a clash between Vietnam and Thailand grew more ominous. Fortunately, no such conflict occurred.

As the Khmer Rouge and the Vietnamese fought a classic guerilla war, their non-Communist neighbors advanced their economies and became rich. The contrast to the poverty of Indochina was beyond endurance for the Vietnamese leadership, in this writer's opinion.

Vietnam's alliance with the Soviet Union yielded few tangible benefits. The overzealous purging of the most talented people in the South after the fall of Saigon resulted in the first tidal wave of boat people, which was a tragedy for Vietnam and America's gain. The intervention in Cambodia placed such a strain on Vietnam's economy that only agricultural reforms in the mid-1980s avoided a collapse.

Complicating the picture further was China's unsuccessful border raid into Vietnam in 1978, in retaliation for Vietnam's intervention in Cambodia. A second tidal wave of boat people from Vietnam followed, which included Vietnamese of Chinese extraction including top members of the Vietnamese Communist Party.

China's policy in Cambodia always had a certain duality. In addition to support of the Khmer Rouge, China backed Prince Norodom Sihanouk, the leader since World War II who was ousted in the U.S.-supported coup in 1970. The Khmer Rouge kept Sihanouk as a figurehead under house arrest except for periodic medical treatment in China, North Korea and Paris.

Prior to his overthrow in 1970, Sihanouk had ruled as a nominally neutral leader, buffeted by the more powerful forces which surrounded him. Relations with the Khmer Rouge had always been difficult. Many of the Khmer Rouge had been taken as children for indoctrination to North Vietnam after the 1954 Geneva Accords which ended the first Indochina War. Others were influenced by their studies in Paris, while many were partial to Mao's Cultural Revolution. Even before their open rebellion in 1967, Sihanouk had been pursuing his Rougies by force.

The encroachment of the Second Indochina War, the "American War", led to the use of eastern Cambodia as a supply line into South Vietnam for the Communist forces of the North. Another serious problem was the advent of the drug trade, from which Sihanouk's French wife, Monique, was rumored to profit. Others wanted their share, and so the beginning of the Cambodian narco-state.

In the face of such tremendous adversity, Sihanouk's survival was miraculous, including his bout with cancer. Sadly, the devastation of Cambodia was nearly complete in the early 1980s.

By the mid-1980s, China's international interests began to shift as its economy and foreign trade moved into high gear. Their commitment to their Khmer Rouge allies, who were incredibly blood thirsty, began to wane. Cambodia's chance to escape from the absolute brink of disaster arrived.

The change in China's foreign policy stemmed from developments in the late 1960s. Mao's Cultural Revolution left China's economy and military in a total shambles. China began to seek out relations with the United States to counterbalance the Soviet Union, with which there were harsh ideological disputes and border clashes.

Richard Nixon, in a 1967 article in Foreign Affairs, a United States quarterly, had offered rapprochement with China. Upon his election to the Presidency in 1968, Nixon moved decisively to deliver on his promise.

As the first term of the Nixon Presidency advanced, his administration sought to use the rapprochement with China as a lever to pressure Vietnam. The consequences of these "divide and rule" tactics were devastating for the people of Indochina.

China and Vietnam had a two thousand-year history of conflict, marked by periodic Chinese invasions. Vietnam was one of the few countries to defeat the Mongolian horde which had occupied China. China's Foreign Minister Chou En-lai, one of the fixtures of Communist rule, had actively pressured Vietnam to accept the 1954 Geneva Accords, which left Vietnam divided.

Vulnerability toward China obsessed the Vietnamese leadership. It was no doubt one of the prime motivations for the North's rush to reunify Vietnam after the 1973 Paris Accords. A more gradual reunification along the lines the Vietnamese

Communists presented prior to the 1973 agreement would have yielded immense economic benefits to their country.

•————————————————————————•

In the wake of the total disarray in Indochina in the aftermath of the "American War", where could the Southeast Asian nations turn? They turned to Japan, which had occupied Southeast Asia during World War II. At the end of the 1960s, Japan had entered the club of advanced developed nations. The tremendous demand created by the United States' war effort in Vietnam was the "icing on the cake" of Japan's miraculous economic boom decade of the 1960s. As a consequence of the peace treaty that ended World War II, Japan was left without an offensive military capability. Though it no longer presented a direct military threat, its neighbors harbored suspicions that Japanese militarist groups would try to repeat their wartime excesses.

Prior to the Paris Agreements of 1973, Japan's diplomacy toward the Southeast Asian nations had remained in the shadow of the American ally. The riots in Indonesia, sparked by the 1973 visit of Japanese Prime Minister Tanaka Kakuei, led to a major effort by Japan to rebuild its relations with the entire region.

Japan's successful economic development offered an inspiration to the members of ASEAN, who welcomed a more Asian approach to development. ASEAN originally asked Japan to help coordinate economic development projects which would benefit all the countries of the region, i.e. the joint manufacture of a regional automobile for which each country would specialize in the manufacture of specific parts. Since all of the ASEAN countries — with the exception of Singapore — were exporters of the same type of raw materials and agricultural products, there was very little trade within the region. This left the ASEAN relationship weak on the economic plane, and, at the diplomatic level, efforts to achieve neutrality were without promise in any way.

Rather than cooperative economic projects, what transpired in Japan's economic relationship with Southeast Asia was the "outsourcing" of manufacturing processes that were labor intensive to the nations of the region.

By the mid-1990s, however, some of the most advanced Japanese technologies and complete industries had left Japan entirely.

In the 1970's, however, Japan's relations with ASEAN were still quite tenuous. Japan was anxious to secure access to oil from Indonesia as part of its plan to reduce dependence on Middle Eastern supplies. Japan's ability to economize and efficiently utilize energy proved more viable than efforts to diversify away from oil as an energy source.

Japan's foreign aid program in the early 1970s had a singular bias toward the development of economic infrastructure, and especially electric power generation. The terms of loans were strict, and there were few outright grants of charity even though some of the aid was Japan's reparations for World War II. As they had only recently developed their economy, the

Japanese understood the nuts and bolts of what a country must do to develop quickly and efficiently. While attacked by Western countries as not "humanistic", Japan's aid helped the Southeast Asian nations to lay a solid foundation for economic development and particularly for the electric generation required to operate Japanese-owned factories.

The creation of an industrial base was a lightning stroke for the ASEAN countries. As their economies boomed and their export grew, they were able to afford armaments for self-defense.

ASEAN's other secret to success was its diplomatic effort to seek rapprochement with China and Vietnam. Trade was the primary motivation. Indonesia had ties with Vietnam which dated from the 1954 Geneva Accords for which it was one of three members of the "International Control Commission" charged with the supervision of the agreement's implementation. Singapore, as a successful, mainly Chinese city-state, was of great interest to China during the era of Deng Xiao-ping.

Through their persistent efforts which capitalized on the acute economic crisis of the Vietnamese as well as on China's new economic direction, it was possible to pierce the veil of hostility and establish a basis for coexistence and trade with their Communist neighbors.

There was another major dividend from ASEAN's efforts — the end of the overt quarrel between Vietnam and China.

This removed tremendous stress on the Southeast Asian region and was of considerable significance for the rest of the world.

Economics was the primary motivation in the rapprochement between Vietnam and China. Both nations had come to realize the advantage of full membership in the world economic club. For Vietnam, an end to the economic burden of the war in Cambodia also made possible membership in ASEAN and access to foreign investment as well as hitherto blocked loans from international financial institutions. In China's case, the devastating international televised coverage of the crushing of the democracy movement at Tien An Men Square in Beijing in 1989 posed vast public relations hurdles.

China's cutoff of aid to the Khmer Rouge in exchange for the withdrawal of Vietnamese troops from Cambodia was, in this writer's opinion, a strategic move to break out of the shadow of Tien An Men.

CONCLUSION

Economics and trade have always been the driving force of China's foreign policy since ancient times, as is recorded in Professor John K. Fairbank's book, "The Chinese World Order."

What is new in this account is the role of economics as the lubricant in the resolution of political and diplomatic disputes. The role of the regional leaders of ASEAN in the diplomatic efforts that led to this great success was nothing short of brilliant.

Their powers of suasion anchored only by their economic success carefully balanced the interests of the concerned parties so as to create a mechanism to actualize those interests jointly. Except for the Khmer Rouge which refused to participate, all parties felt that they were winners.

Economics is not an antidote to politics and ideology. However, its balm can work wonders. In their wisdom, the leaders of ASEAN have set an important precedent for the settlement of disputes that stem from the colonial period.

CHAPTER TWO

HOW CAN WE ACTUALIZE THE link between politics and economics in the diplomacy of the Twenty-first Century?

There can be no unique approach, but the outline of a formula could be as follows: The international community must view each dispute in its full political, economic, historical, and cultural context. Only then can there be an assessment as to the factors that might facilitate a resolution.

The peoples of the nations involved can play an important role in the resolution of the dispute. Information is the key in this regard.

Leading countries in each region can play an important role, or perhaps friendly outsiders will help out. Where there is a shortage of political muscle, the art of suasion will have to be highly developed.

The following is an account of several dispute resolution situations, mostly in Asia, for which the political-economic linkup has been put in various stages of motion. The strong points and limitations of this approach in the context of each situation merit considerable attention. The more familiar the international community becomes with this approach, the more successful it can be in the future, in this writer's opinion.

KOREA

In 1993-4, the Republic of Korea (South Korea), the Democratic People's Republic of Korea (North Korea), the United States, China, and Japan came to the brink of conflict regarding North Korea's nuclear capability. The United States insisted that North Korea was assembling its own independent nuclear arsenal through the use of spent nuclear fuel from its Soviet-made nuclear power plants and test reactors. The United States was actively contemplating attacks on this arsenal. In addition, North Korea had been developing its own ballistic missile capability, apparently with the financial assistance of several Middle Eastern countries.

An independent North Korean nuclear arsenal would quickly prompt its much-hated neighbor Japan, with the world's largest stockpile of plutonium, to develop its own nuclear arsenal. The consequence of a Japanese nuclear arsenal would be too awesome to contemplate.

The negotiations with North Korea remained at an impasse, as North Korea clumsily attempted to maneuver the United States into a position to deal with it exclusively on the reconfiguration of a cease-fire arrangement that had been in force for forty years. The North Koreans refused to include the

South Koreans who had not been directly a party to the original armistice agreement.

The traditional diplomatic route had reached a dead end. Was there another approach? Could a regional approach tied to North Korea's economic needs transcend the intramural Korean bickering? As South Korea's economy had prospered mightily, North Korea's economy had contracted with major financial consequences. North Korea was desperately short of electric power generation capability even to run its obsolescent factories.

If China, Japan, the United States, and South Korea jointly created a regional organization to promote the resolution of North Korea's energy problem, perhaps North Korea would be more amenable to a political settlement. As part of the agreement to create "KEDO", the Korean Energy Development Organization, the North Koreans had agreed to engage in negotiations with the South, which had undertaken a five billion dollar burden to install the new light power reactors in North Korea. The progress toward these negotiations has been painful but inexorable.

In addition to its economic crisis, North Korea suffered devastating flooding in 1995 and then again in 1996, which left large segments of the population without food. Mid-1997 would mark the peak of the crisis, in the view of experts.

China did not participate in "KEDO", but it gave its sanction to the regional approach. China had continued to maintain close ties with North Korea, but, over a certain limit, it required payment in cash which North Korea did not have. Turbulence in North Korea would reverberate badly in the border area with China, which had a substantial Korean minority of its own. The Koreans nurse territorial claims against China.

China had already established diplomatic relations with South Korea, whose industrialists had been pouring investments into China. Dynamic and aggressive, the South Koreans offered China a counterbalance to Japan. The "China Card" will surely play a major role in the resolution of the Korea problem as well as in the structure of relations in Northeast Asia.

It should be totally obvious that too many political perils exist to assume that economic factors alone can be instrumental in the resolution of the Korea problem. North Korea had arisen as a state under the most adverse circumstances imaginable, but it had a unified leadership at that time. Even with a clean succession to the deceist founding leader Kim Il-sung, it was far from clear that North Korea could rise to meet the challenges.

In this writer's view, there is a strong need for a Northeast Asia Development Organization, embracing at the minimum China, Russia, Japan, and North and South Korea. Only by involving all nations of the area in a regional development effort can Northeast Asia achieve a threshold for peaceful coexistence. Under such an umbrella, internal developments in North Korea are most likely to develop harmoniously.

China and Taiwan

In 1976, the Republic of China (Taiwan) and the People's Republic of China (China) agreed to seek a peaceful rapprochement. It was the first step toward reconciliation since the Nationalist government fled to Taiwan after its defeat by the Communists in 1949. By 1976, it was already clear to both parties that China would soon modernize and seek reentry into the world economic order.

In Chinese history, there were precedents for negotiations between contending parties even without resolution of the "sovereignty" issue. In his essay in the book, "The Chinese World Order," Professor Benjamin Schwartz recounted negotiations during the era of the Southern Sung during which the negotiators faced "East-West", since to stand "North-South" would acknowledge the sovereignty of the Northern party. In China, only the Emperor faces South.

By 1976, Taiwan's economy had progressed brilliantly. The government had managed its affairs well. It had inherited a good economic infrastructure and a fine educational system from the Japanese colonial power. In the 1980s, Taiwan developed a high-tech infrastructure and a booming computer parts industry, which developed into an advanced computer industry in the 1990s. Along with Singapore, Taiwan joined the ranks of the developed nations in the 1990s.

As this economic progress occurred, another important development emerged: the Chiang family, and specifically

Chiang Ching-kuo, son of China's World War II leader Chiang Kai-shek, laid the basis for Taiwan's transition to Western-style democracy. In 1976 the prospect of democracy in Taiwan seemed as distant as China's emergence from the cauldron of the Cultural Revolution to become a modern, industrialized country.

The 1976 death of Mao Zedong, China's leader, brought to an end the "Great Proletarian Cultural Revolution," Mao's decade-long effort to exorcise China's past and cultural traditions. Even as the Cultural Revolution shook China to its roots, pressures began to mount from outside the country. China's economy fell into disarray, and its military became ensnared in factional rivalries. China developed a pressing need to seek relations with the United States in order to counterbalance its rapidly deteriorating relations with the Soviet Union.

As early as 1974, articles appeared in the Chinese press regarding the sage Confucius during whose lifetime China made the transition from the Bronze Age to the Iron Age. Four years later, the age of Soviet-inspired obsolescence and self-inflicted economic ruin was to give way to a new high tech rebirth and an economic boom under the leadership of Deng Xiao-ping. In the intervening four years, power struggles raged in the Chinese leadership as Mao's wife and her cohorts grasped futilely for power. The casualties were reportedly staggering.

Although a participant in the "Long March", the 1933-4 escape from Nationalist encirclement which was the definitive event in the establishment of Mao's leadership over the entire Communist Party, Deng Xiao-ping had experienced numerous reversals since the founding of the People's Republic in 1949. He had been purged for excessive pragmatism and tenacity.

Nevertheless, Deng Xiao-ping had retained strong ties to the military, which had suffered badly during the chaos of the Cultural Revolution. During his leadership in the period after 1978, the military formed various corporations both to advance its influence but also to cover its own expenses. Chastened by the 1978 defeat in the border war with Vietnam, Deng sought to bring the military along with the economy to the level of parity with the advanced nations by the early Twenty-first Century, no small goal.

Deng's strategy was to provide incentives for foreign investment in the coastal areas, especially when such investment involved the introduction of new technologies. With China's ample supply of cheap labor, foreign companies and overseas Chinese investors flocked in, despite numerous obstacles caused by China's lack of a legal tradition.

As had been the age-old pattern in China, economic imbalances arose during Deng's modernization campaign between city and countryside as well as between the coastal areas, which received subsidies to promote foreign investment, and the inland areas. Restive and over-taxed, China's farmers grew unwilling to be bound to the land, which was often taken away from them arbitrarily by officials. These are the familiar lyrics to the strains of Chinese history.

Demarcated by the June 1989 events at Tien An Men Square in Beijing, the succession to Deng Xiao-ping moved to center stage, as the determinant to China's political fortunes. A Shanghai group rose to the ascendancy under the leadership of Jiang Zemin.

Territorial disputes simmered with neighboring countries as China's sudden economic power raised the level of fear among its neighbors. The Sengoku/Tiao Yu Tai dispute with Japan and the Spratly/Paracel and South China Sea Continental Shelf dispute with the Southeast Asian countries, particularly Vietnam, continued to fester.

Relations with Taiwan had developed mainly on the economic plain, as Taiwanese investors poured vast sums into southern China. They outsourced labor intensive industries to take advantage of not only China's cheap labor but its considerable market potential. Sometimes investments were made through the United States subsidiaries of these Taiwanese companies. As time passes, the Taiwanese government has become increasingly nervous regarding the growing importance that market share in China has come to assume for Taiwanese companies.

Conversely, China's new leadership watched with the greatest anxiety as Taiwan successfully carried out democratic elections in the spring of 1996. These elections marked the end of the post-1949 dominance of the Chinese mainland elite. They confirmed in power Lee Teng-hui, a native Taiwanese. China launched naval exercises in the Straits of Taiwan in

March 1996, but these only appeared to help Lee's chances. However, the popularity of the pro-Taiwanese Independence faction appeared to diminish.

Even as economic ties have strengthened, the intramural diplomatic wrangling between China and Taiwan has continued unabated. In this writer's opinion, both sides need to demonstrate a bolder vision of the future. They need to undertake joint projects at the international level to promote the development of poorer nations. A "Marshall Plan" for the new states of Central Asia may be the key to the removal of instability for that region. China and Taiwan should join the Southeast Asian countries in the joint development of the oil resources of the South China Sea, the proceeds from which should be directed to regional development according to an equitable formula.

As beneficiaries of the world's export markets, China and Taiwan have to do their share to help their neighbors. Only such an approach is worthy of the spirit of modern China's founding leaders, in this writer's opinion.

China's political and economic structure is still at least a generation out of phase with Taiwan's. Over time the two parties will evolve a more durable relationship. In the meantime, the force of reason is the only power that will yield positive developments in relations between China and Taiwan.

THE MIDDLE EAST

Since World War II, no other part of the world has lost its economic edge more than the Middle East. Rapid population growth combined with economic stagnation, an unlimited arms race and the destabilizing effects of various wars including the Arab-Israeli conflict have caused a severe drag on the advancement of the region.

Regional efforts to promote economic development and the rational use of water resources have languished.

The current peace efforts began after the defeat of Iraq in the 1991 Gulf War. At that time, the key players reached a consensus that war no longer presented a viable alternative, and they initiated contacts themselves to promote a peace settlement. Before the painful memories of the Gulf War give way to even more painful events, it is the task of the international community to ensure a lasting commitment to peace by the parties.

Selective adherence to the Oslo Agreement has been the rule. Perhaps the words "land for peace" need a clearer definition. It will take time for the parties to work that out among themselves. In the meantime, they need only look at the success of the East and Southeast Asian nations to see what the future of peace can be.

All of the nations of the Middle East need to be brought into the peace process, including Iraq and Iran. Short term economic boycotts inflict pain, but they don't teach "lessons". Peace needs to be incentivized: first, according to the rules of the United Nations Charter, and second according to the rules of the "world economic club."

Even as it defies the United States, Iran has busily developed transportation and trade links with its neighbors. With its burgeoning population and diminishing natural resource base, Iran faces a dilemma. Will it trade-in its aspirations for regional hegemony and to be gadfly to the United States in exchange for full participation in the "world economic club" and regional development efforts?

To achieve the "politics of inclusion", the leaders of the area will have to be more effective in rousing their populaces to support the peace process. This is the true test of leadership. A return to war would be devastating for all concerned.

BOSNIA AND THE EX-SOVIET BLOC

The sudden collapse of the former Soviet Union, its allies and the other related states of Eastern Europe has brought a tremendous disarray, a veritable Pandora's Box of economic, political, and ethnic disputes.

Countries with stronger Western traditions, including the Czech Republic, Hungary, and Poland, have found the transition to be less onerous. The other states have had to adjust not only to capitalism but also to democracy. Ethnic disputes, the curse of history, have been allowed to run amok. Preoccupied by the Iraqi invasion of Kuwait, the international community was a mere bystander as events in Bosnia unfolded.

In many of the formerly socialist states, a "new class" has emerged from amidst the previous era's "new class" of party bureaucrats and the military elite. The "new, new class" has appropriated for itself the assets of the previous socialist states, much of which it has secreted abroad.

The international community needs a more proactive approach to deal with these nations. The expectations of the populace can have an important influence on the political leaderships.

With the rise of xenophobia and deportations in Western Europe, emigration is no longer an option.

In the case of Serbia, the populace finds itself noticeably poorer — by 90%, according to estimates — since the beginning of the Bosnian War. If the Serbian populace wants to enjoy the "normal" Western-style life to which it aspires, it will have to influence its leaders to play by the rules of the "world economic club." The international community must actively inform the Serbian populace and the other Balkan peoples of the necessary facts of life of international relations.

Into the post-Cold War diplomatic quiver, there must be a new array of stategems and economic incentives. As was the experience of the Marshall Plan in Western Europe after World War II, foreign aid can only contribute in a meaningful way to a society in an atmosphere of self-help. Where the Communist system and ethnic conflict have shredded the economic base of a country, the task of rebuilding — or building — will be long and difficult.

The international community needs to sharpen its expertise in regard to the effective denationalization of state assets, and as to how to equitably distribute those assets among the populace and away from the hands of gangsters.

Where assets are too concentrated or have fallen into the wrong hands, strategies exist to redistribute them. When the Nationalist regime fled to Taiwan, it initiated land reform and redistribution through compensation of landowners with long term, low interest bonds. These bonds acted as the collateral base for investments in industry that have made Taiwan one of the most successful economies of the world. Of course, Taiwan's success was largely contingent on economic stability.

The international community must help these post-Socialist nations secure their economic base so as to promote political stability. A body of civil and commercial law is a prerequisite for progress. An informed populace is the key to success.

CONCLUSION

Economic factors add an extra dimension to each of the political disputes mentioned in this chapter. This naturally reflects the aspirations of countries and peoples to advance themselves and their fortunes. The task of diplomacy in the

23

Twenty-first Century will be to "fine-tune" these aspirations in a way that will mesh with the overall goals of the international community. The creation of regional frameworks may help to take the bite out of intramural disputes; in addition, there is the possibility that a new sense of purpose may arise to replace the old antagonisms. Too often, these antagonisms have arisen as a result of the crush of historic events, over which none of the parties thereto have had any influence, except as the victims. As the victims, it is so easy to lose sight of the true causes of the victimization. Hopefully, the information revolution which is sweeping the world will help to resolve this situation.

CHAPTER THREE

EVEN AS THE GLOBAL ECONOMY has become increasingly integrated, structural weaknesses in any country's economy can have serious implications for the rest of the world. Let us consider the case of Japan.

Since the 1970s, Japan's economic powerhouse has progressively integrated itself with East and Southeast Asia. Japanese corporate investment has stimulated an unprecedented prosperity throughout the region, which has become an important supplier of manufactured products to the rest of the world.

New technologies are as likely to originate in the "overseas" subsidiaries as in the "home" Japanese plant.

Nevertheless, a certain reserve remains in the Asian attitude toward Japan, partly as a consequence of Japan's actions during World War II. What would boost the confidence of Japan's neighbors? The short answer appears to be: greater openness and transparency in Japan's internal affairs.

Like its other trading partners, Japan's neighbors want to

sell it more. They and many others would like to know the source of Japan's current economic malaise. Let us make a quick examination.

Japan's economic problems are crystallized in a singular occurrence in the Fall 1996 election campaign. Severe criticism from every political direction was targeted at the Ministry of Finance, because of the economic malaise. The awesome powers of the Ministry of Finance, which include control over the budgets of all the other ministries as well as supervision of the banks and financial markets, have proven ineffective in the face of real interest rates which have long since dropped below zero. How could Japan have gotten itself in such a severe situation?

In its frenetic rush to rebuild Japan's economy after World War II, the financial structure of the economy did not develop evenly. Japan's economic bureaucracy selected key industries for development, which it subsidized with low interest loans from the banking sector. The economic surplus which made these loans possible was generated by the low tech industries, thus "shifting the burden" (shiwayose). Once the key industries were in place, the economic bureaucracy did not modify the financial structure to be more flexible so as to promote new industries. The automobile industry defied the bureaucrats, but it was the exception.

A short historical detour is necessary to explain the position of the bureaucracy in the Japanese government, which is different from the West. Fifteen hundred years ago, even before

China's cultural influence became predominant and in particular the role of Confucianism, the primary role of government in Japan was the proper ordering of ancestral records. With the opening to the West in 1867, the role of Japan's bureaucrats was to arrange the imported institutions of the West in such a way as to preserve the orderliness of society.

Today, the complexity of Japan's international position has sorely tested the bureaucratic structure. No matter how rich a country may be, its wellbeing can drastically diminish if its economic institutions fall out of step with the rest of the world.

The current economic situation in Japan reminds this writer of a Kabuki play which fails to culminate. Imagine the brightly clad star, who has changed his costume again and again on stage with the help of a team of inconspicuous helpers, so as to preserve the forward thrust of the drama which combines dance with dialogue. The star strains again and again to prove his true faith at the moment of truth, the shonenba. Alas, it is of no use.

To end this long pause, Japan's financial policy is in need of a mid-course correction, assisted by some inconspicuously clad financial advisers. In essence there are three key areas which require immediate attention: financial and capital markets, land policy, and the procedure for consolidating subsidiaries into the balance sheets of the parent corporations.

First, in the area of financial markets, Japan's stock market suffers from the general perception that it is unfair and inefficient. Investors require access to a wide range of investment vehicles — stocks, bonds, etc. — which they can trade without fear of market manipulation.

At the root of the stock market's problem is the vast over-concentration of up to 80% of the shares of the major corporations, banks, and insurance companies outside of the marketplace. Although these insiders hoped to ward off foreign takeovers of Japanese companies by sterilizing such a large portion of the shares outside of normal trading, trading in the remaining 20% of outstanding shares has been "thin" and thus at the mercy of the market manipulators.

As stock prices dropped in unison in the early 1990s, the position of the key corporate players weakened. Finally, in the summer of 1996, they agreed to gradually reduce the "close holdings".

In the meantime, however, the inefficient Nikkei stock index has been a mouth-watering target for international speculators, which has had a further destabilizing influence.

In regard to long term capital markets, Japan's regulators have given absolute preference to only the most blue chip issuers of corporate debt. Except in government bonds, secondary bond markets barely exist in Japan. The "less favored" corporations have to take their bond issues to the Euromarkets, where Japanese investors snap up 90% of the Yen-denominated issues. What an irony! Japan, the world's major supplier of capital for over twenty years, sends its corporations to the Euromarkets to raise capital from Japanese investors.

The creation of free, fair, and efficient financial and capital markets is something which is easily in Japan's reach.

The second major issue for Japan's economic reform is land policy. Even as Japan's financial markets did not develop efficiently, Japanese land prices soared from the end of World War II until the early 1990s. While land prices were rising, tax policy discouraged sales, as the annual assessments were mild in comparison to the extremely high tax rate at the time of land sales. The permissible use of land as collateral for loans added to the speculative frenzy. When the Bank of Japan finally tightened credit in the early 1990s, land prices sank along with stock prices.

Since the major corporate players had large landholdings in addition to large holdings of each other's stocks, they were caught in the squeeze. The Japanese banks had to borrow capital from abroad to meet the capital sufficiency standards of the Bank for International Settlements. Bank lending to individuals diminished, and those who had the misfortune to inherit or who had to raise sums quickly found it necessary to sell their properties at bargain prices. In many instances, they simply handed their lands over to the tax collector. Companies had to quickly liquidate foreign holdings at a substantial loss to cover domestic obligations.

The priorities of Japan's tax policy need reassessment. In

any event, land should not qualify as collateral for bank loans. Only the marketplace can devise strategies to deal with the land problem.

Some of the speculative frenzy in regard to land may be fed by the actions of the banks which do not compete on a level playing field with the Government's Postal Savings, for which consumers do not have to pay tax on interest earned on savings accounts.

The third critical aspect of Japan's economic dilemma is perhaps the most critical. Without accurate and complete financial statements, Japan's financial and capital markets cannot function efficiently. The key flaw is the failure to fully consolidate all subsidiaries and related companies into the financial statement of the parent corporation. If Japan adhered to "International Accounting Standards" which are comparable to "GAAP" rules in the United States (Generally Accepted Accounting Principles), then the current financial crisis may have been avoided. In particular, an extremely complex legal framework complicates the transition to International Accounting Standards, as pointed out by Professor Hiramatsu of Kansai Gakuin University.

If procedures for consolidating financial statements had been adequate, it would not have been possible to disguise losses in land company subsidiaries of banks as well as losses on land held as collateral in "distant" bank branches, which was especially the case in Western Japan (Kansai) including areas affected by the 1995 earthquake.

As a result of inadequate accounting controls, organized criminals — the Yakuza — were able to muscle into the operations of the land investment companies and bank branches. When the parent banks belatedly became aware of the magnitude of the problem, the Yakuza shot and killed the auditors.

A number of the large Japanese "City" Banks had been in the process of bringing the accounts of their main offices in line with the accounting system in the main United States banks — i.e. Citibank. But what of their subsidiary branches?

Observers often compare the current Japanese banking crisis to the 1980s savings and loan crisis in the United States. There is one primary difference: due to stricter accounting standards, it was finally possible to plumb the depths of the losses in the savings and loans, despite numerous political complications. The 1990s banking crisis in Japan will not resolve itself so easily.

[Addendum note: On June 6, 1997, the Japanese Government announced its intention to institute international standards for consolidated financial statements, according to the Nihon Keizai Shinbun newspaper of June 7, 1997.]

CONCLUSION

Capitalism in Japan dates from eight hundred years ago. It has always adapted itself to the needs of each era, from feudal lords to corporate conglomerates. More transparency in Japan's financial affairs will eventually untangle the current

"Gordian knot". This development will instill confidence in Japan's neighbors and trading partners.

A major test of the "world economic club" will be how it addresses the implementation of "International Accounting Standards". Without reliable financial statistics, confidence will not exist.

The 1990s experience in Japan is the manifestation of a latent situation, whose resolution will have to be worked out by financial experts.

Chapter Four

Is there a pattern of Peacemaking which can replace Great Power enforcement? Can the rule of the "world economic club" come to bear in such a way as to enforce conformance to international norms?

The "world economic club" has to become more adept at bringing the power of interlocking economic relationships to bear in a dynamic way to influence events. Nations will surely retain their sovereignty for generations to come, but they will find themselves increasingly intertwined with others, near and far. How can this reality be transformed into a force for peace and harmony?

In this chapter, let us first review some of the difficulties encountered in the application of economic strategies to the resolution of political problems, i.e. backsliding. Then, let us look at the application of the economic approach to peacemaking to a different crisis situation.

The Backsliders

Economic necessity — and not adherence to international

norms — is the prime motivator in many conflict situations. Once there is a turn toward peace, it is the task of the international community to leverage that turn into something more tangible and long term. As part of a settlement, it is necessary to tap into the power of public opinion in the affected nations to create a constituency for peace and an understanding of the benefits that peace can provide — i.e. membership in the "world economic club".

There is no cudgel with which to pound every country which chooses to deviate from the prescribed course. Rather, the international community needs to have a steady hand to hold the course and then to secure the desired result.

CAMBODIA

Cambodia's travails are far from over. Racked by infighting in the current ruling coalition, the situation is tenuous. Only a restoration of the economy shattered by years of Khmer Rouge rule can help reestablish stability. The scourge of narco-trafficking is another serious problem.

It is not sufficient for the international financial institutions to threaten to withhold loans from Cambodia until it brings the illegal lumber exports under control. Rather, it is necessary to develop a plan to make this possible, and to ensure that the importers of these logs cooperate.

The rehabilitation of countries with shattered economies will be a major long term headache for the international community for generations to come.

Vietnam

Vietnam's turn toward participation in the "world economic club" has been substantial, but it has a long way to go. Generations hardened by war may not be able to easily grasp the subtleties of the new situation. It may be easier for Vietnam to achieve economic rapprochement with its neighbors before it can play a full role on the world scene. Ironically, this may put Vietnam at a decided disadvantage as compared to its northern neighbor, China.

International aid should aim to put in place the basic economic infrastructure in Vietnam. Time is playing its role on the aging leadership. Will the new leaders be ready to make the important choices? The moment of truth is not far off.

Israel

The international community has actively promoted the peace process between Israel and its neighbors. Now it is the time for the international community to encourage Israel to make important financial reforms commensurate with its new status as an advanced economy.

Like many new members of the club of advanced economies, Israel's banking sector is weak and vulnerable, in this writer's opinion.

Yitzhak Rabin, the former Prime Minister who was assassinated, reportedly was trying to implement regulations to curb money laundering. Although the media attributes the motives of his assassin to hatred of the Oslo Peace Accords with the Palestinians, it is not clear that that is the final word on the subject.

Rabin's successor, Binyamin Netanyahu, was the first prime minister to be elected by direct popular vote, rather than selection by his political party. Netanyahu owes his election to support from the influx of refugees, mostly Jewish, from the former Soviet Union. A number of these refugees are conducting money laundering on a vast scale, according to press reports.

What will Netanyahu do to strengthen the banking sector and to resolve the money laundering problem?

It is not enough to be elected as a political leader in the world as it exists today. It is also important to put in place the proper internal safeguards to protect the internal political process from contamination.

Insidious forces, perhaps long tolerated for cozy political reasons, may make a sudden grab for power. Other new members of the club of advanced nations and those who aspire to that status should review their own situation in this regard.

Iʀᴀǫ

After its successful buildup of its war machine thanks to a network of dummy companies throughout Western Europe and the United States, Iraq marched into Kuwait with ease. Will it be tempted to repeat the error of its ways? Now that Iraq has acceded to the United Nations terms for oil sales to finance humanitarian aid for its people and reparations for the victims of its war, no one can truly believe that Saddam Hussein has learned a "lesson". Rather, it appears that the Baghdad government wants to make business deals.

The task of the international community will be to set up controls and oversight to ensure that Saddam hews to the rules of international behavior. Saddam needs a clear road map, so that there is no ambiguity in regard to the consequences of any indiscretions. In the complex business environment of our era, the international community faces a daunting task.

Inevitably, Iraq will have to reintegrate into the world economy. The challenge is to make it do so on the terms of the "world economic club", not on its own terms.

Tʜᴇ Nᴇxᴛ Cʜᴀʟʟᴇɴɢᴇ

How can the nations of a region join together with the international community to deal with a persistent crisis? No one better than a neighbor knows the special conditions and historical problems involved. That is precisely the reason that

ASEAN (Association of South East Asian Nations) had so much success dealing with its Indochinese neighbors.

The United Nations could be more effective in the resolution of these regional disputes. Up to now, the U.N. has functioned as a "fire wall" to hold back the flames and to shelter the refugees until the member nations could decide on a strategy to deal with the crisis. Sadly, at times there has been no strategy at all.

Many members blame the U.N.'s failure to do more on the domination of the five World War II powers in the Security Council.

The real problem, in this writer's view, is the shortage of dynamic players at the "medium" power level who have the will and motivation to play a dynamic role in the resolution of regional disputes. As trade booms and more nations take advantage of the technological revolution to build up their economies, there will be a greater potential supply of nations which can perform these new roles.

Let us consider a simplistic scenario which combines the role of regional leaders with an international effort to resolve the dispute in South Asia between India and Pakistan.

The border between India and Pakistan is one of the two hottest flashpoints in the world today. If the United States, Russia, and China provide security guarantees against nuclear attack to both India and Pakistan in return for full disclosure and United Nations inspection of their nuclear deterrents, that should set the tone for a general lessening of tensions.

A regional combination between ASEAN and the South Asian nations in the form of a "free trade zone" might be the next important step. With the exception of Pakistan, India has already formed favorable trade relations with its neighbors. Pakistan has demanded a resolution of the Kashmir dispute in advance of any commercial relationship of this type.

President Nelson Mandela of South Africa has proposed an association of nations on the rim of the Indian Ocean. His proposal might also be helpful in this regard.

In this writer's view, the most likely regional players would be Singapore, which is already an active investor in India's high tech industries, and Malaysia, whose high-profile leader, Mahathir Mohamad, has shown himself to be resourceful and ambitious.

Are these countries ready for the challenge?

Can constructive economic interaction create a new plane of interests which makes it possible to finesse tensions in other areas? What of the expectations of the populace of the affected nations?

Before the colonization of India, Hindus and Moslems coexisted in peace. How can this situation be restored?

The economic truncation of the Indian Subcontinent at independence has been a source of great misfortune. Pakistan needs stronger economic ties with India to cope with its booming population and sagging infrastructure. An unstable Pakistan is a real menace to India. If Pakistan should fall under the control of an "Islamic Fundamentalist" leader, tolerance of the large Muslim minority in India might reach its limits, as seen by the recent riots in Mumbai (Bombay).

India has recently cracked the door of its economy to foreign investment. It needs to pursue the free market approach with greater vigor. A less insular approach to the international community should yield a more broadminded approach to its regional relationships.

While the borders established at the time of partition are unlikely to change for strategic reasons, a "super-autonomy" for Kashmir would be more likely to succeed in the context of enhanced economic interchange between India and Pakistan. According to this logic, economic intercourse would act as the "consideration" for the improvement in political relations.

The international community, through the United Nations, should set up an oversight forum to ensure that all of the parties do not try to undermine the new understandings. There must be a price of admission and a price of continued benefits. Economic and financial reform should also be on the table. Without clear lines of accountability, the effort to combine peacemaking with an international security umbrella is not likely to succeed.

CONCLUSION

In today's world, membership in the "world economic club" is the primary inducement for nations to conduct themselves according to international norms.

The "insecurity of nations" and the arms race will always be a factor. The price of war and conflict has to be looked at as the loss of benefits that accrue to members in good standing of the "world economic club". Even Saddam Hussein appears to have signed on to this "benefits of peace" approach.

What can the international community do to capitalize on its strength? It needs to play its "diversity" card to the maximum. With a more dynamic role for regional leaders, conflicts may lend themselves to more durable solutions.

CHAPTER FIVE

AS THE ONLY REMAINING SUPERPOWER, how can the United States expand its foreign policy role beyond that of "spear carrier"?

As a nation built on a base of diverse peoples who share common values, diversity is the core strength that the United States possesses. Now is the time to adapt the talent for managing diversity to the construction of a new platform for international relations, which will include a wide range of partners around the globe who share core values.

As a corollary to its ability to manage diversity is the second major strength of the United States: the openness of society and the enterprising spirit to overcome weaknesses and correct mistakes.

Now is the time to fine tune these strengths to turn them into crucial selling points in foreign relations.

The ceaseless effort to open markets abroad is the first step toward this new policy of "managing diversity". Where the technologies are irresistible, there will be ultimate success. For example, in February 1997, there was a major breakthrough in the opening of world telecommunications markets. In March 1997, thirty-nine nations agreed to drop tariffs on computers and other information related products.

To maximize this policy, the United States must seek to make the spirit of openness infectious enough to convince other nations to grapple with their own internal situation so as to reap the fruits of openness. While the United States' view of "democracy" and "human rights" may not be universally popular, it is plain for all to see that openness to change is a crucial element for survival and prosperity in the Twenty-first Century. As nations grow more accustomed to openness, their internal body politick will evolve accordingly.

Southern India is exemplary of this new situation. This region has become a primary supplier of software to the world. With their newly earned wages, software programmers can buy their own home computers, which have virtually a limitless ability to communicate around the globe. Demand for the finest computer equipment must be extraordinary, so as to stay competitive. Therefore, it is apparent that market liberalization in the areas of telecommunications and computer equipment is inexorable.

To advance to the next foreign policy frontier, the United States must "market" its policy to the needs of other countries. Thus the United States must rouse itself to be more aware of their needs. Blessed with tranquility, the United States has to come to grips with the complexities of the rest of the world.

Except for the financial media, the public is largely uninformed on world affairs.

The worst case example of the media's failure to keep the public informed is the case of Iran prior to the fall of the Shah in the late 1970s. While the British Broadcasting Corporation reported in detail on a daily basis, the U.S. media was oblivious. It is no wonder that the hostage crisis at the U.S. Embassy in Teheran was such a shock to the public. This shock has had a long term impact on the approach that the United States has taken toward Iran.

The media needs to keep the public informed on the new opportunities for business that the open trading system has made possible. This will provide an outlet for those whose jobs disappear as a result of free trade, and it will enable the rest of the populace to prepare to qualify itself for the new opportunities.

One important benefit from better public awareness of foreign affairs could be the reduction in the need for the Executive Branch to resort to the use of force in the event of sudden crises. Today's military is better prepared to cope with crises and near-crises, especially the humanitarian relief situations. However, it is wrong to lean on the military's skills excessively, and it is unclear that their skill alone will be adequate to meet future challenges.

In the new foreign policy of diversity, the United States needs to move from the Cold War concept of "containment" to a new plane of policy called "engagement with accountability" which would utilize the levers of the "world economic club", i.e. the price of entry and continued membership, to enforce compliance.

The areas of compliance are almost countless: conformance to the United Nations Charter; participation in the World Trade Organization; cooperation in the suppression of the drug trade and money laundering, etc.

All countries must understand that they cannot enjoy the benefits unless they are willing to shoulder their share of the "world economic club's" burden.

In economics, this problem is called the "free rider" problem. Of course, the issue is how to exact a "fee for services" on these parties.

A major dilemma for "free trade" has been government intervention to assist and subsidize their own national companies. Such dirigisme — or government-led economies — has been a thorn in the side of those who advocate trade liberalization. While it is not possible to directly counter the popularity of dirigisme, it is possible to create a climate whereby one country's dirigisme will cancel out another's. For example, in 1996, Japanese automobile manufacturers could no longer export their cars to Indonesia which had begun working with a Korean company to market a "national" car. Japan now finds it necessary to protest to the World Trade Organization. This is a great opportunity for the United States to press Japan to open its markets further. How better to make Japan's case in the World Trade Organization more convincing?

The new United States foreign policy will not work in isolation from an improvement in domestic affairs, which was the major casualty of the Cold War. The low educational level of the general public and the decline of health standards, despite the rapid escalation of health care costs, are among the most glaring problems. The absence of preventative care and the increase in drug addiction and AIDS are problems of the greatest urgency, along with crime and the decline of the basic physical infrastructure. A country's population is its most important resource. No country can afford to alienate or subsidize its citizenry.

A return to basics in domestic policy will convince other countries that democracy works in the United States.

CONCLUSION

As the only remaining superpower, the United States will still have burdens to bear for the rest of the world. It should advance its role from that of "spear carrier" to that of a concerned big brother. The "spear" can change forms. It is as likely to be the Voice of America rebroadcasting Belgrade Radio B-92 as it is an aircraft carrier on duty in the Adriatic Sea. Or, perhaps the battle will be waged on the Internet, the computerized battlefield for "hearts and minds".

Better communication and the spread of information need to be the primary goals of policy. And not coincidentally, there must be a greater sophistication in regard to helping countries become accustomed to the open flow of information. This will be a task of the greatest diplomacy.

The more "traditional" a society, the harder the adaptation will be.

On a direct, bilateral basis, the United States must be perfectly clear that our partners may not abuse the benefits of free trade. The NAFTA agreement with Mexico is a primary case in point, in particular the 1994 crisis. At that time, privileged insiders distorted the country's financial statistics to their own favor, with devastating consequences to the value of the peso and to the economy in general. In classic "beggar they neighbor" form, Mexico's exports soared and imports dropped sharply. The general public was victimized in both countries.

While the Clinton administration was correct to help finance Mexico's recovery from the crisis, it needs to be more blunt on the subject of the "level playing field". The Mexicans seem to be playing as if free trade was the old Aztec ball game in which the losers are executed. The financial machinations of Mexican insiders have offered an engraved invitation to powerful thugs — including the drug barons — to muscle aside the politicians so as to gain control of the nerve centers of the country. In such a privileged position, they can do incalculable damage to the international financial system and to the "world economic club".

The United States needs to welcome a diversity of views which add vitality to its circle of allies, but it needs to select its partners with the greatest care.

The United States itself has been the beneficiary of such diversity already. Despite trade friction with Japan, the manufacturing and management methods learned from Japan in the 1980s helped reenergize the United States' industry in the 1990s.

Rather than view every challenge as a menace, Washington needs to adopt the point of view that it is time to let some fresh air into the Board of Directors room. The old "good versus evil" approach makes great Hollywood movies, but it does not address the realities of the post-Cold War environment. "Containment" must give way to "engagement with accountability".

A more collegial approach has already produced good results in world affairs, as shown by the arrangement (modus vivendi) worked out by the Southeast Asian nations after the end of the "American War" in Vietnam. Their success shows that mutual self-interest and the rules of the "world economic club" can coincide harmoniously.

This reformulation of diplomacy strikingly resembles the recent reinterpretation of the "business cycle" in economic theory. Traditionally, economic theory predicted that economies traverse a boom and bust cycle. Wages and prices soar as the boom develops. When the economy nears full utilization of its productive capacity, the bubble bursts with the result that wages and prices plummet.

However, in an environment of progressively freer trade, the availability of inexpensive imports acts to prevent sharp price increases and thus counteracts any outbreak of inflation. Similarly, the economy is prevented from reaching the limits of its capacity.

In this light, the concrete value of free trade does not lie only or even primarily in restricting the prices for products. Rather, with more stable price levels, the suitable environment is caused to exist whereby new industries and opportunities arise which can expand the range of opportunity for everyone.

Therefore, the more intimate nations become with each other economically, the more likely the remaining barriers to trade will fall down. Other types of barriers are likely to come down with them.

"Engagement with accountability" assumes that the "world economic club" will enforce stiff rules of entry and continued membership.

The United States can help lead the way to this brighter future.

— April, 1997

Index